I0100344

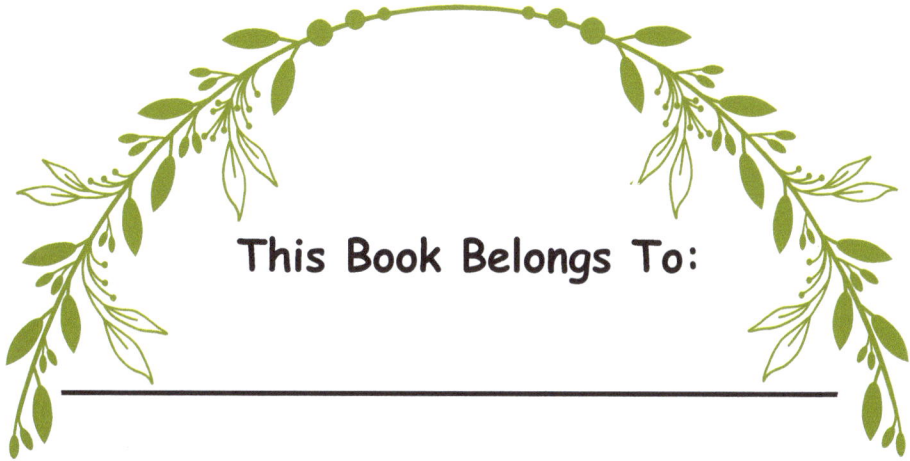

This Book Belongs To:

_____

Presented By:

On:

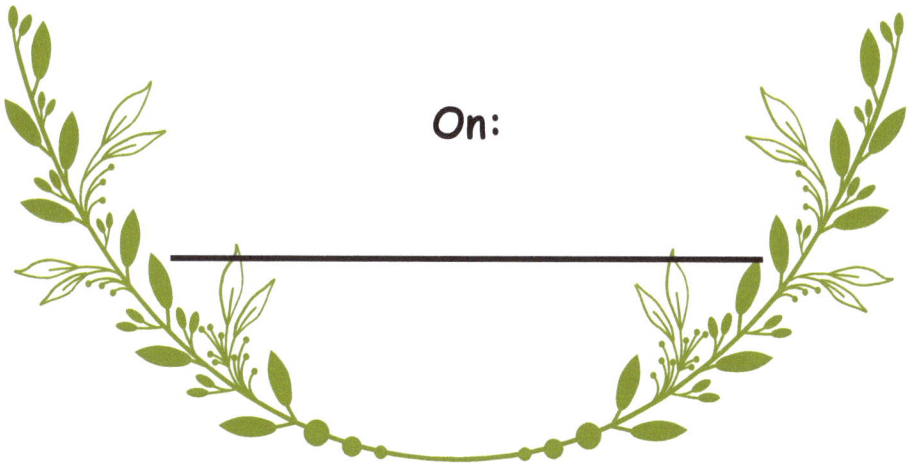

This book is dedicated to our three grandchildren: Reid "The Engineer," Quinn "The Music Man," and Lauren "The Creative One." Without them, our lives would be way less fun!

This is a work of non-fiction. Please note the information contained within this document is for educational and entertainment purposes only. All effort has been executed to present accurate, up to date, and reliable, information. The content within this book has been derived from various sources.
All Scripture quotes are taken from the
New Living Translation except where noted.

Copyright © 2024 by Janice Millane Wasmer

All rights reserved. No part of this book may be reproduced or used in any manner without written permission of the copyright owner except for the use of quotations in a book review. For more information, address: wildartamerica@gmail.com

Revised Hardback Edition August 2024

Book design by Janice Millane Wasmer WildArtAmerica Publishing. Special thanks and appreciation to my two editor-daughters, Janelle L. Channell and Renaya G. Van Dusen. Without their loving support, encouragement, and editing this book for me, this endeavor would have been much more difficult.
Furthermore, I would like to thank my husband, Ed Wasmer, who
supports me and my art in every human way possible. To him, I am most grateful.

ISBN 979-8-9907327-3-5 Hardback

www.janicemillanewasmer.com

In God's Creation
Animals of the Forest
A Book for "Kids" of All Ages

Written and Illustrated by Janice Millane Wasmer

This book culminates a decade of wanting to create a children's book. It was "God-breathed" from its inception. I wanted to develop a series of wildlife paintings about three years ago and paint them in my favorite "kid style." I never put together in my mind that these paintings would be used just for this purpose. But God knew! Isn't it amazing how He knows how to orchestrate our lives? For me, it happens all too often in my creative world. He gives me inspiration at night, usually when I cannot sleep. A thought or a vision will come into my mind suddenly. I have learned to keep a small notebook by my bed for such occasions. I hate stumbling out of bed when I get one of these ideas. So having something to write on close by is a lifesaver! I love all of God's creation, and I wanted to share my interpretation of it. This book is about God's creation and forest animals. I want to write about all of the general animal habitats God created. This is the first in a series. I hope you and your children enjoy this book for many years.

"My thoughts are nothing like your thoughts," says the Lord. "And my ways are far beyond anything you could imagine." Isaiah 55:8

In God's Creation
Animals of the Forest
A Book for "Kids" of All Ages

"The heavens proclaim the Glory of God. The skies display his craftsmanship." Psalm 19:1

Deep in the forest, in God's great creation, many creatures live. From the smallest ant to the biggest bear, they each have their place and their purpose. For God loves them all and will forever provide them with abundant food, fresh water, and crispy clean air. He watches over them with His love and His care.

"I know every bird on the mountains, and all the animals of the field are mine," Psalm 50:11.

As we follow the path the tiny ant makes, or we wander along the animal trails, there is life and wonder to be found under every leaf or blade of grass, in God's forest lands. Behind every bush or up the highest tree, something to see, something to hear. What do you see? What do you hear? Even the smallest ant to the biggest bear. They live their purpose in God's creation.

"When you open your hand, you satisfy the hunger and thirst of every living thing." Psalm 145:16

When one looks at nature, how can one not see God in it? This is a question frequently asked by those who believe. From the depths of the sea to the mountains so immense, for in the truth of God's being, there is no pretense.

"For ever since the creation of the world, His invisible attributes, His eternal power and divine nature, have been clearly seen, being understood through His workmanship [all His creation, the wonderful things that He has made], so that they [who fail to believe and trust in Him] are without excuse and without defense." Romans 1:20 AMP

"But Jesus replied, "Foxes have dens to live in, and the birds have nests, but the Son of Man has no place even to lay his head." Luke 9:58

In God's beautiful creation, one crazy-eyed fox is close to me. Frolicking through flowers, delightful is she. She jumps and runs, twirls and rolls, is light as a feather and is quick on her toes. The next thing I looked, she was leaping a brook off into the sunset in the little time she took.

"There the owl will make her nest and lay her eggs. She will hatch her young and cover them with her wings." Isaiah 34:15

In God's glorious creation, whether bright day or dark night, there are so many creatures; it is such a great sight. To look down in the grass or up in a nest, a mommy and baby, not a single night's rest. Observing for movement, they scope, and they watch. While other raptors are sleeping, they search for a catch.

"Be strong in the Lord and in his mighty power." Ephesians 6:10

In God's wonderful creation, we often find mysterious wonders of every kind. A beautiful elk who maneuvers through trees in the dark forest silently with ease. Oh, look! Those antlers! So big and so strong! He bumps into nothing as he travels along. How wonderful! How magnificent! What a creature he is—powerful yet agile. These attributes are his.

"Your righteousness is like the mighty mountains, your justice like the ocean depths." Psalm 36:6

In God's awesome creation, in the mountains, sea, or land, all creatures are stirred by His mighty hand. The lynx is a cat, as curious as can be. She saunters through landscapes that humans rarely see. She masterfully climbs the trees and the rocks, while the long fur on her paws makes her feet look like socks. She hunts mostly the sick and the weak, so she is called an "orderly of the forest." She stalks her prey with the skill of the smartest.

"For I can do everything through Christ, who gives me strength."
Philippians 4:13.

In God's creative creation, how great can it be? Our God is a master of the land and the sea. He even created the great grizzly! The most massive of creatures, by might as he wishes, He scouts thrashing waters in search of the fishes.

"As the deer longs for streams of water, so I long for you, Oh God!"   Psalm 42:1

"So don't worry about these things, saying, 'What will we eat? What will we drink? What will we wear?'
These things dominate the thoughts of unbelievers, but your heavenly Father already knows all your needs.'"   Matthew 6: 31-32

In God's incredible creation, far in the field, are a doe and her fawn as they feast on the yield. The Creator provides the grass and the wheat to forever provide for the meek and the beast. And yes! God loves even them. For all creatures depend on air, water, and food. And the earth that God made provides all that is good.

"Look at the birds. They don't plant or harvest or store food in barns, for your heavenly Father feeds them. And aren't you far more valuable to him than they are?" Matthew 6:26

In God's magnificent creation, with grass, they build. Low in the bushes are their nests, neat and skilled. The beautiful red cardinal with his brown mate for life sworn. He feasts on sweet seeds, berries, and corn. Daddy takes over after the babies are born, while Mommy flies off to build their next home.

"The name of the Lord is a strong fortress;
the godly run to him and are safe." Proverbs 10:10

In God's immense creation, a coyote is here. So smart and so cunning, but never too near. His nickname is "Song Dog", and he's an excellent swimmer. He can make many sounds, whether it's a bark, yip, scream, or growl. He is the guardian of the forest, but sometimes will scowl, to warn any intruders to back off and leave! He is establishing territory or a mate to retrieve.

"The thief's purpose is to steal and kill and destroy. My purpose is to give them a rich and satisfying life." John 10:10

In God's amazing creation, here we can find two "hanging out" friends, five fingers on each hand. They dip each morsel of food in water, then to a new neighborhood to become the next squatter. They go through the trash with cunning and care, then off they go running, to us unaware.

"Shout joyful praises to God, all the earth!" Psalm 66:1

In God's bountiful creation, isn't it funny, a small little creature called a rabbit, hare, or bunny? When a rabbit is happy, he leaps, twists, and kicks, all slinky. This is known as a "binky." A rabbit's teeth never stop growing! They are worn down as the rabbit keeps chewing. A rabbit will purr when relaxed and happy, but what do you think is its best feature? It's the very long ears of this cutest little creature!

"For through Him, God created everything in the heavenly realms and on earth. He made the things we can see and the things we can't see such as thrones, kingdoms, rulers, and authorities in the unseen world. Everything was created through Him and for Him." Colossians 1:16

In God's stunning creation, a moose you might see, swimming in water for miles with glee. Moose loves to swim, and underwater, they go, holding their breath for 30 seconds or more. They look for their food in rivers and lakes, but don't run from a moose; you'll never make it. For 35 miles an hour, they can run, give or take it.

"You are worthy, O Lord our God, to receive glory and honor and power. For you created all things, and they exist because you created what you pleased." Revelation 4:11

In God's beloved creation, squirrels build nests or live in holes in trees. They scamper to the ground for nuts, fruits, or seeds. Ground squirrels live in burrows under the ground. You will always see squirrels scampering around. Their sense of smell is so powerful that they can find food a foot under the snow. Because of constant gnawing, their front teeth always grow.

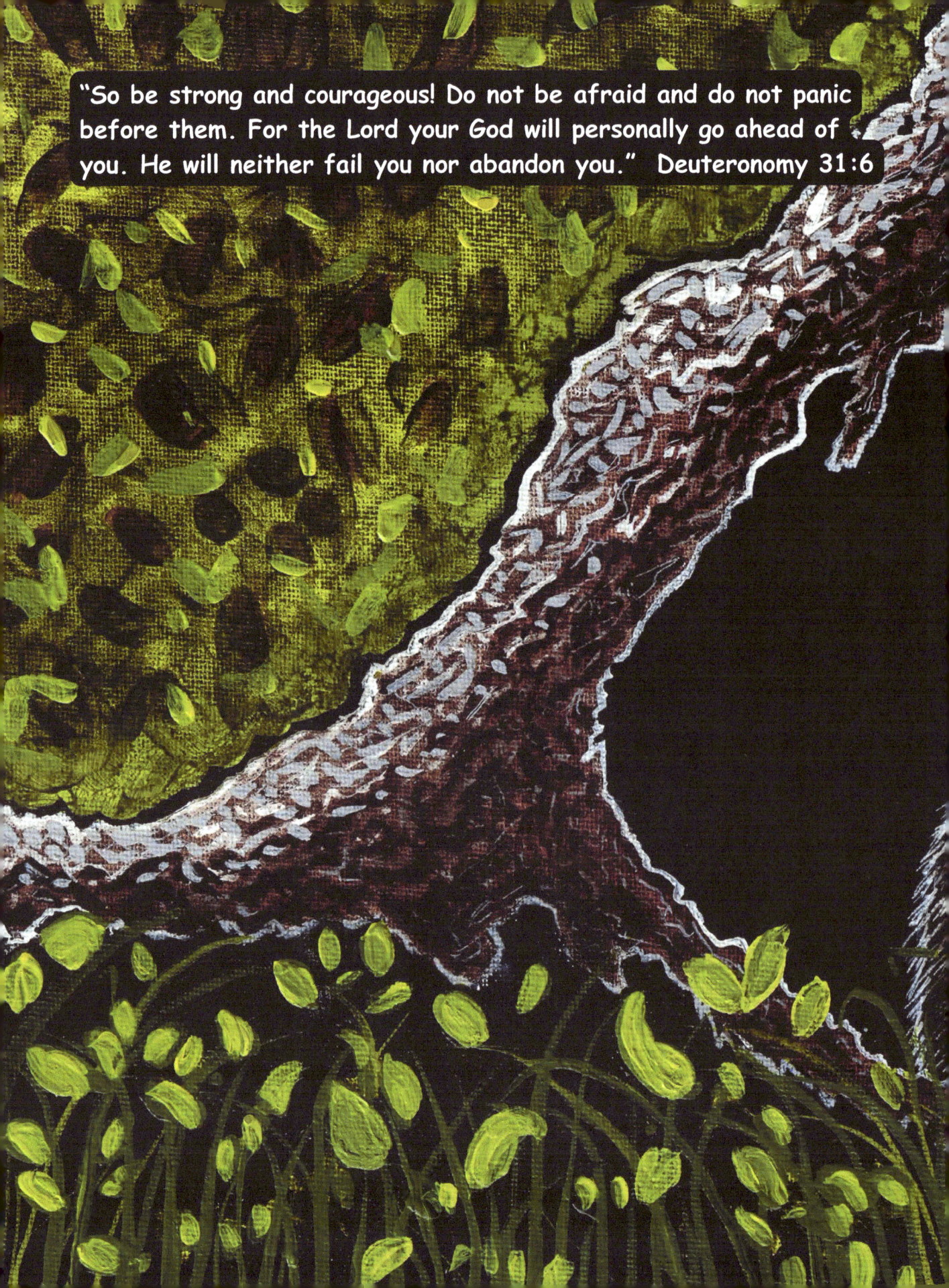

"So be strong and courageous! Do not be afraid and do not panic before them. For the Lord your God will personally go ahead of you. He will neither fail you nor abandon you." Deuteronomy 31:6

In God's marvelous creation, in an underground tunnel, a brave badger sleeps for two days. This is just one of her curious ways. She will wake up to eat and then sleep some more. This peculiar behavior is called "torpor." Badgers are shy, but do not let that fool you. She is known to fight off even the largest of foes with her very long claws attached to her toes. Don't mess with a badger; this is a fair warning. Just let her sleep 'till late in the morning.

"For I know the plans I have for you," says the Lord. "They are plans for good and not for disaster, to give you a future and a hope." Jeremiah 29:11

In God's brilliant creation lives a smelly little skunk that can target its spray from over 12 feet away. Some species of skunk do a handstand to spray, putting their warning markings on full display. If the person or animal doesn't retreat, the skunk aims the spray, and the skunk will "beat feet." The spray can remain on its target for days.

"He made all the stars—the Bear and Orion, the Pleiades and the constellations of the southern sky. He does great things too marvelous to understand. He performs countless miracles."
Job 9: 9-10

In God's **excellent** creation, of colors black, red, and white, is the mighty bear. And yes, it can have different-colored hair. Called an "omnivore," they eat both plants and small mammals. Bears can run as fast as camels. Don't feed the bears, as we all know from the signs, or they will forever be in your trash cans.

"He fills my life with good things. My youth is renewed like the eagle's!" Psalm 103:5

"But those who trust in the Lord will find new strength. They will soar high on wings like eagles. They will run and not grow weary. They will walk and not faint." Isaiah 40:31

In God's majestic creation, above in the sky, the bald eagle soars, flying higher than high. Its head is not bald, but "balde" as in white. It belongs to the family of hawks, vultures, and kites. With sharp talons wide open, it seeks its next meal. Its image is on America's Great Seal.

But one of the twenty-four elders said to me, 'Stop weeping! Look, the Lion of the tribe of Judah, the heir to David's throne, has won the victory. He is worthy to open the scroll and its seven seals.'" Revelation 5:5

In God's powerful creation, a great hunter prowls. Its territory can be one hundred square miles. Its dark gold eyes shine green at night. Weighing up to 200 pounds, the mountain lion's presence can cause a fright! The toughest of animals, it hisses, grunts, and purrs. But one thing is for sure, it does not roar.

"You can go to bed without fear; you will lie down and sleep soundly."
Proverbs 3:24

In God's astounding creation, in the forest habitat, lives another large feline called the bobcat. These wild cats are known for their sharp claws, distinctive black spots, and powerful jaws. They are nocturnal, which means they are up most at night. They sleep in their dens, curled up, snug, and tight.

"My sheep listen to my voice; I know them, and they follow me."
John 10:27

In God's splendorous Creation, in the forested mountains, live the agile bighorn sheep. They traverse the mountains so high and steep, butting their heads with a crash and a tumble, fighting for dominance, they cause a great rumble. They love to eat green grass and clover. They are known for their large horns all over the world.

"Look, I am sending you out as sheep among wolves. So be as shrewd as snakes and harmless as doves."   Matthew 10:16

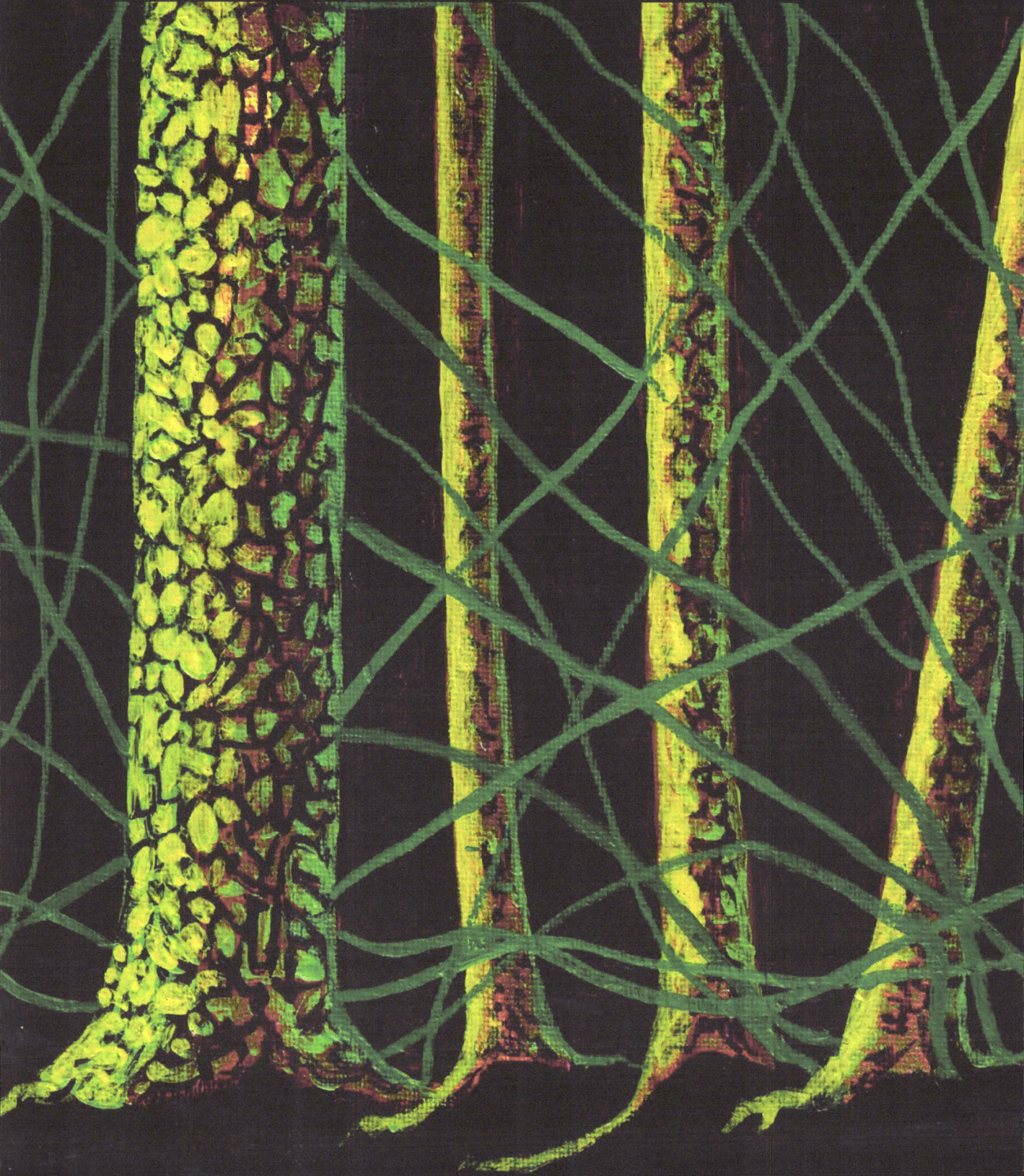

In God's blessed creation, in the dark of the night, lies a tired grey wolf—and oh! What a sight! From five miles away, its powerful sense of smell is a human being whose scent he knows well. Crossing paths with a wolf is one rarely crossed. They avoid humans in nature at almost all costs!

In God's **divine** Creation, there is always a plan. His love is eternal for all His "kids", woman and man. He loves all of His creatures; you can tell. For God, our Creator blesses all so well. So this story must end but do not despair, for the world God made with His splendor and care is yours to explore, to wander and enjoy, For God so loved the whole world and all His Creation. He watches us all, nation to nation. So be happy, rejoice! And never forget that God, YOUR Creator, is not done with YOU yet! For He wishes to see your purpose fulfilled, in this generation, in you, His glory, instilled.

"For this is how God loved the world: He gave his one and only Son, so that everyone who believes in him will not perish but have eternal life." John 3:16

www.ingramcontent.com/pod-product-compliance
Lightning Source LLC
Chambersburg PA
CBHW041548260326
41914CB00016B/1585